The Sacrifice

*A year in the life of a Regional Field Director
on the Obama Campaign for President*

By
Douglas Wilson, MHA

LEGACY HOUSE
PUBLISHING GROUP

Published in Orlando, Florida, by Legacy House Publishing Group. www.LegacyHousePublishingGroup.com

ISBN: 978-1484879672

TABLE OF CONTENTS

SECTION 1

MY STORY

CHAPTER 1

THE CALLING OF A NEW DAY

February 10, 2007 was a day that most Americans will remember. I can recall the day very well. I was in Rock Hill, South Carolina visiting my girlfriend. It was like any typical February day....cool and sunny. At this time, I was 28 years old with a Masters Degree in Health Administration and was working for a healthcare firm. I was not happy. I was looking for a way to make a difference in the lives of people.

The country was in the middle of a new political season. There were many good Democratic candidates on the ticket, which made the choice for a nominee difficult. I thought to myself two things: "What kind of name is Barack Obama?" and "Is this just another black candidate?" Like most Democrats, I was planning to support Hillary Clinton but there was something that kept drawing me to Senator Obama. When he spoke, his words reflected everything that I believed in. I also understood his multicultural background. My father is from Jamaica and my mother is from Panama. Yet, even with all of this; I was still not ready to support the Senator until February 10th.

I remember the moment very well. It was eleven o'clock at night and I was sitting on the edge of my bed. I didn't get a chance to see Senator Obama's speech earlier that day so I decided to watch it on CSPAN. As I watched I was in awe. The day seemed very cold but yet bright. The old Illinois State Capital was still full of its strength and manor. I was also amazed at the large crowd. Their faces were filled with the type of joy you see on those of children on Christmas morning.

They came from all parts of the country --- some as far as Maine and Florida --- just to see one man. Some people stood on cars. Others placed their young children on their shoulders so they could see history in the making. The day was so cold, that I could see the breath of people coming from their mouths. Then without a moment's notice, the crowd erupted in a thunderous cheer, and out walked a tall and slender, handsome Senator with a Kennedy-like swagger. His family was beautiful and enchanting.

The people in the crowd held up shiny blue "Obama 08" placards. These signs reflected the very tenacity and elegance of the soon to be presidential candidate. Senator Obama, along with his family, waved at the crowd with big smiles and a spirit of confidence. After a few waves and handshakes, he proceeded to the podium. He approached it with elegance yet also with a spirit of humility. As he looked down at the speech in which he was about to deliver, I could see the look of determination and strength in his face. As he began to speak, I could feel myself connecting to and understanding every word he spoke. I finally had a feeling of hope that if elected; he would do away with the overwhelming partisanship of Washington.

In his speech, one of the things that Senator Obama stated was his desire to build a more perfect union. When finished his speech, I was filled with a new sense of hope and obligation. I said to myself on that day --- February 10, 2007 --- that I would do everything I could to help elect Senator Barack Obama as the 44th President of the United States.

The next day I went back to work in Charlotte with the speech on my mind. I had never worked for (or even volunteered for) a presidential candidate before. However, I could not help but feel the overwhelming call to give up all that I was doing to help out the Senator. The only issue I had is that I was currently employed at a healthcare firm called The Lash Group. Before joining the Lash Group, I had a very tough time trying to find employment. I had graduated from the University of South Carolina just six years prior, in May of 2001. Like most college graduates, I felt like I owned the world, but was very quickly disappointed. I believed that I would receive a job making $60,000 a year and everything would be fine. The summer after I graduated, I spent every day feverishly searching for employment. I had doors slammed in my face and was told that I didn't have enough experience. It was one of the worst things I had ever experienced at that time.

Finally in August of 2001, I received a call from the Lash Group Healthcare Consultants. This would become my first job out of college and in the span of five years; I would end up leaving the company and returning again. So here I was in 2007 trying to decide whether or not I should leave the company again to go and work for Obama.

One night, while driving to visit my parents in Camden, South Carolina I decided to call my good friend, Anton Gunn. Anton was one of the few men that I knew who dedicated his life to helping others. As I drove down the dark road of Interstate 77, I picked up my phone to call him. To my surprise, he answered his phone; in which he usually does not due to a hectic schedule. I told him that I saw Senator Obama give his announcement speech and that I wanted to help out. He told me that he was actually hired by Obama himself to serve as his Political Director in South Carolina. He encouraged me to be the Rock Hill Lead Volunteer for Obama. Without hesitation, I accepted the task to spread Obama's message of hope and change.

My first task as a volunteer was to form an organizational meeting for key community leaders in the Rock Hill Area. Anton asked me to send him a list of these names. I made some calls to my pastor and others in Rock Hill to try to figure out who the best individuals would be. I was amazed somewhat to the fact that when I explained to my contacts why I needed these names, they thought I was crazy. They did not know who Barack Obama was and felt like it was just too early for him to be campaigning. They also thought he did not have a snow ball chance of winning the Democratic Primary. Nonetheless I still pushed forward in my quest to have the Organizational Meeting.

9

I was able to get through to a well known businessman in Rock Hill named Melvin Poole. He gave me a list of approximately 100 people. I gave the list to Anton and was then given the task of finding a location for the event. I immediately suggested the Freedom Center. The Freedom Center was one of the largest facilities in Rock Hill. It was a multi-purpose 6500 square foot facility located in the downtown area. It also housed the church that I attended at that time, Freedom Temple Ministries. I figured this would be a good opportunity for the Freedom Center and the members of the church to experience and get involved in this new political process.

I set the date for early March of 2007. I was very excited about this event because I felt that this was my chance to really show the community why Obama should be president. I told some of my colleagues at work about my new endeavors. Some were excited. Others took me as a joke. This is something that I would experience for the next two years.

We called numerous leaders in the Rock Hill Community. To my dismay, only ten people showed up. I was shocked at this low turnout. I would later learn that in organizing, your first meeting will usually have a low turn out. After the meeting, I felt that I might have blown my chance at becoming a part of the Obama campaign. However, I truly believed in my heart that if I worked hard, I would be able to introduce the world to this great leader.

During the meeting, I learned a great deal about the Senator. The presenter, Laurin Manning gave a true depiction of Obama in very few words. It wasthe perfect sales pitch, and a strategy that would be used to win the White House. The next day, I received a call from the South Carolina Political Director, Anton Gunn. He informed me that the Campaign wanted me to do a presentation about Obama to the York County Democratic Party. They were impressed with the way I organized the Freedom Center Event. I accepted the task.

York County, South Carolina is home to the 5th Congressional District. The Congressman for this district, John Spratt, was one of the most powerful politicians in Washington. He was the chairman of House Budget Committee. Having this knowledge caused me to feel even more hesitation. Albeit I knew I would do a good job during the presentation, I was still a stranger to this new exciting Senator.

The meeting was held at a restaurant in the City of York. It had a very distinctive name, the Coal Yard. I was very uptight about the location. It was a home-style restaurant located in a very conservative town. Secondly, I was given the historic opportunity to talk about the presidential campaign of an African American. Although the country and the South have made enormous strides in race relations, there were still ghosts of America's Dark Past. I picked myself up and accepted what I believed to be a daunting task. At 5:30 p.m. on that spring day, I drove thirty miles from Charlotte, North Carolina to York, South Carolina.

I arrived ten minutes early at the restaurant. To my surprise, the attendees were already seated and ready for my presentation. I was told to sit at the head of the table. After a hefty serving of sweet potato fries, I began my presentation. I started to share with them what Obama meant to me. I explained that I viewed his story as the true American Dream. He defied all odds that were against him. He grew up without a father. His mother raised him but eventually passed away from cancer. This would greatly shape his life, as well as his political career. I also spoke about how Obama desired for his campaign to be a part of America. This very gesture was not only an inspiration to me but to many Americans. I went on to explain his stance on bread and butter issues such as Education, Healthcare, and The War in Iraq.

After my presentation, a sense of urgency filled the room. Some members were ready to join the movement. Others were still hesitant but drawn to Obama's story. Nonetheless, the pitch had been made and the time had come. I called my soon to be boss and told him: *"Jeremy, I am ready to join the O'Train!"*

CHAPTER 2

JOINING THE O'TRAIN

Going back to work the next day proved to be very difficult. One thing that I knew throughout my life is that I wanted to help change the world one issue at a time. The meeting in York showed me that the only way to make this possible was to give up my life of comfort and dedicate my time to Senator Obama. As I sat at my desk, I looked out the window and gazed at the water fountain. I knew that I would miss this view greatly. I watched the power of the fountain and all its entire splendor. The powerful rays of the sun reflected on the fountain with the same strength that I saw in the Senator. I also had a splendid view of the Charlotte-Douglas Airport. While I was gazing upon the fountain I caught a glimpse of a plane taking off. As I watched the plane, I couldn't help but to wonder how much the lives of the people aboard it would change if I succeeded in my quest to help elect Mr. Obama.

I proceeded to type my letter of resignation in which I was about to give for the second time. It was almost like breaking up with someone twice in a row. I tried my best in the letter to express my gratitude to the company as well as why I was leaving. I was very worried about resigning. The Lash Group was very gracious in hiring me back after I left in 2002. Nonetheless, I knew what was best for me and what was best for the country. Although I was not enlisting in the military, I believed in my soul that working on the Obama Campaign would be a service to the country.

I walked to my manager's office and handed her my letter. Courtney McCullough by far was one of the best managers I have ever had. She is a very strong woman who is dedicated to her life and family. Her office reflected every inch and passion of her heart. Her desk displayed pictures of her son and her mother who passed some time ago. One thing that I admired about her was that she believed in me and always knew that I would amount to some type of greatness. She looked over the letter and began to smile. "Barack Obama huh? I am very proud of you." She stated she was not surprised that I was entering the political world. A couple of days later many of my colleagues hosted a series of going away parties for me. One of my closet colleagues, Beverly Southern, hosted a going away party for me at a restaurant named Wild Wing Café. It was one of the best going away parties I have ever had.

On May 30, 2007 I drove down to Columbia, South Carolina to participate in the new staff training. I didn't know what to expect. I was both in a state of utopia as well as a state of fear. The training was being held at Benedict College, which is one of the most prestigious historically black colleges in the country. The training took place in the Swinton Student Center, which was a fairly new facility.

As I entered the room, I realized how cold it was. Notwithstanding the fact that it was about one hundred degrees outside, I was still cold. I was surrounded by fifteen energetic young people. These were people just like me --- people who believed in Senator Obama and were willing to give up their lives (not physically) for him. To my amazement, I was one of the oldest field organizers in the room. I was 28 years old. Most of the field organizers were between 19 and 24. Some had already worked on three or four campaigns before working on this one. I was one of the few that came with no campaign experience.

I recognized some of the other organizers in the room. Travis Johnson was a young politico from Aiken, South Carolina. I remembered him from our NAACP college days. He was very talented and understood the political process. Jeremy Bird gave him the same position as myself, Lead Field Organizer. The room was set up perfectly for a historic presentation. We were welcomed by a series of important figures that would help drive the campaign in South Carolina.

14

Anton Gunn, the Political Director, Stacy Brayboy, the State Director, and of course Jeremy Bird, the State Field Director. They were all well equipped with Blackberries and laptops. They all had the glow of the DC Arena, as well the passion of community organizers.

During the presentation, we learned about who the Senator was and what he believed in. We were also introduced to the community building block called Community Organizing. It was a very uncanny but amazing vehicle. The whole basis of organizing was building leadership by forming personal relationships. Our whole task was to get Obama elected and build a grassroots movement that would outlive the campaign.

I was given the task of building a volunteer base in the Rock Hill Region of South Carolina. This consisted of York, Chester, and Lancaster Counties. As I received this daunting task, I felt my heart drop from my chest to my feet. I was not sure if I could handle the overwhelming stress that was being presented to me. However, I accepted the task and said goodbye to the corporate world and hello to the world of Obama.

Section 2

HOW ONE MAN CHANGED SOUTH CAROLINA

CHAPTER 3

"BUILDING THE GRASSROOTS MOVEMENT"

I arrived back in Rock Hill with a mission to change the way politics was done. However, I was not too sure about the gargantuan; yet uncanny field plan. I was tasked with meeting community leaders in York, Chester, and Lancaster and trying to form a movement that would outlive the Senator's campaign. To my advantage, I was from the area and knew some key community leaders. I set up my first meeting with a woman by the name of Linda Hart. Linda was a very interesting and energetic Irish-Catholic woman. Linda was from the Kennedy era. She was among the youth who were ingratiated in a positive way by the Kennedy brothers.

We met on a bright spring day in early June at her residence in Tega Cay, South Carolina. The town of Tega Cay represented a mix of northern retirees with progressive ideas and middle-aged, southern retirees with conservative ideas. Ms. Hart lived in a lake house at the bottom of a steep hill. When she emerged from her house, a broad smile appeared on her face. She had a green shirt that had Obama's name spelled as an Irish name, O'bama. She enthusiastically invited me into her house, which had the distinct aura of democrat with a liberal Kennedy past.

I was very impressed with her home. It was decorated with plaques from her husband's music producing days. Gold and platinum records hung on the wall, along with pictures with him and famous artists from the glory days of music. As we sat down to talk about the house meeting strategy she offered me some iced tea. Her Boston-Irish accent was rich with Kennedy pride and history.

Linda Hart considered herself a Democratic fundraiser. She proudly told me how she had raised money for many candidates and was in the process of doing a fundraiser for the Senator. She had already contacted the fundraising department in Chicago and they told her that she would have to raise a certain amount of money to meet the campaign goal for that month. I was very excited when I heard this because in my eyes I knew she had the experience and tenacity to accomplish the task, so I began to explain to her how the house meeting strategy works.

A house meeting is a social gathering of supporters at an individual's place of residence or recreation, held to discuss and execute campaign strategies. At these meetings we share stories that give insight into why we want to be be involved in the campaign. We also discuss how a grassroots organization can be formed through a house meeting. For example, if one attendee who came to Linda's house meeting decided to conduct a meeting of their own, and a person who attended that person's house meeting held one of their own, a grassroots movement would be started.

Her eyes lit up with amazement and awe when she heard this. The passion that she had for Senator Obama before we talked had now tripled. She began to list for me all the people that she knew --- everyone from business owners to disgruntled democrats who had lost faith in the political process up until now. She guaranteed that her house meeting would serve as an example for all in York County. I left the house filled with excitement and at the same time disbelief. I was excited because I was in competition with the other field organizers across the state, and I was now able to set up one of my first house meetings. I was also in disbelief because I was not sure if Linda would be able to deliver the number of people that she had promised.

Nonetheless I began working to make this house meeting a success. I followed up with Linda to see how many people she had contacted. "Doug I have contacted everyone I know and it looks like we will have a pretty good turn out," she said. I began to feel much better about this turn out. I also asked her if she could turn out some volunteers for our June 9th Canvass, "Walk for Change". Linda with her positive and lively voice told me "Doug, we will have them there too!" Walk for Change was going to be a nationwide door- to-door canvass in which we would try to generate supporters for the Senator. During this event, we would also push his policy on the Iraq War --- a war he believed (as well as us) was an injust war.

The next day I continued to work out of the York County Democratic Party Office. I was fortunate to be utilizing this space especially during a Democratic Primary. One of our tasks each day was to make 100 phone calls to voters in our region. These calls came from an enhanced data base called the Voter File or VAN. The VAN was an uncanny tool. It contained every single registered voter in the region. It also displayed their demographics and which party they voted for in the last election. We were given a very hard task. We had to cold call these voters and garner their support for the Senator. We also had to ask them if they would like to canvass on June 9th. This was very hard for me. I was in some ways shy so I didn't like to cold call at all. Also, this was my first time phone banking and I wasn't sure how to conduct one. I was also very much aware of the fact that many people did not have any idea who this man was [Obama].

We had a system as to how to code voters when we spoke to them. If they supported the Senator we would mark them as a 2. If they were undecided they would be a 3. If they were for Senator Clinton, we marked them as a 4 and so forth. As I called voters, to my dismay many did not even want to discuss politics with me. However, there were some who actually knew him and expressed their support for him. I was able to reach my goal every day of making 100 calls, but my contact rate (how many people I actually talked to) was pretty low. I would learn later that the reason for this was because I was calling individuals 55 and younger instead of seniors.

I was unsuccessful securing a decent amount of volunteers for June 9th from my phone banking so I referred to my warm market (individuals I knew from church, the local party, and Linda Hart's inner circle.) As June 9th approached I was a nervous wreck. I only had five people confirmed. We had to knock on at least 150 doors. Our state goal was 500 doors. I worked tirelessly on the phones and my warm market. I did not want to let Anton down. He put his neck out for me when he told JB to hire me. I also did not want to ruin the only chance in history to help elect the first African American President.

A week before the June 9th canvass we had a trial run in Columbia with the whole staff. Jeremy broke us up into groups of two. I and another organizer by the name of Derrick Nayo went to a community in North Columbia. I was more terrified then than in any other time in my life. I had no idea what to say once someone came to the door. I also was afraid of rejection.

Off we went to North Columbia. Derrick rode with me. As I parked my car, my stomach was in knots. I asked Derrick if I could watch him do a couple houses before I would go on my own. After a few houses together, I decided to go on my own. The first house I approached was a Caucasian man in his late fifties; early sixties. I rang the door bell full of nervousness and self confidence. The man came to the door, took one look at me, and then slammed the door in my face. This was my first experience of canvassing and this same reaction would happen to me time and time again throughout the campaign.

The rejection of this individual shook my confidence to the core. Nonetheless, I gathered myself and kept going. I came across another home where a woman was working on her garden. She was a Caucasian woman in her fifties. Her appearance was peaceful and reminded me of the stories of the Kennedy Democrats of the 1960s. As I approached, she laid her garden tools down and smiled at me. "Hello" she stated with jubilance. "Hi' I replied back. I am a field organizer with Senator Barack Obama's Campaign for President. I am going door to door today talking to your neighbors about Senator Obama's campaign and his Iraq War Policy." "Wonderful!" she replied.

She went on to tell me how much of a supporter of the Senator she was. She signed our supporter card and wanted to volunteer. I finally received my confidence back. I was ready to go on to my next house. As I began to walk, I realized that the one element of politics which is the most important is the grass roots. Many campaigns neglect the field aspect and focus only on money and political outreach.

The next voter I spoke to was an African American male in his mid-forties. "What's up bro?" he asked. I told him that I was with the Senator's Campaign. "Honestly," he replied "I don't think he is going to win" Heck, I don't even think he is black." This response not only baffled me, it made me very upset. I began to reflect on my days at Camden High School in Camden, South Carolina. Many blacks who rode the school bus with me would call me white. They would say that because of my light brown skin and the size of my house that I was white. This voter began a long story of the reason why he supported Senator Clinton, which was because of Former President Clinton. He also gave me a very disappointing explanation as to why he believed that the Former President was more "black" then Senator Obama. He stated that because the Former President had oral sex while in the White House, this made him more of a black man. I walked away in disgust after his dour comment. The rest of the evening I walked house to house talking with voters and listening to their concerns. I received a first glimpse of the true America. Americans were in pain and desired real change more than ever before.

After the canvass we came back to the Columbia office. Everyone was excited about their results. I, for one was not very pleased with my own. I felt that I had failed the Senator, especially when my other teammates had higher numbers. I knew that canvassing would be hard for me going forward. I had to make sure that I recruited as many volunteers as possible to make June 9th in Rock Hill to be the best. Afterwards Jeremy directed us to the supply room to pick up materials for the canvass. We had water, handouts and the other key materials needed for a successful canvass. I left the Columbia office timid but at the same time ready to tackle the next task at hand.

June 9th! The day had finally come. It was a very hot Carolina summer day. The temperature was 96 degrees; one of the hottest days of the year. I arrived at the Freedom Center at eight in the morning. I waited with anxiety to see how many volunteers would actually arrive. I called Monique Perry, my Deputy Field Director, to report in. Monique was a young energetic woman from Michigan. Although she was small in stature, she was a force to be reckoned with. It was getting close to 10:00 a.m. the time for volunteers to show up. The Freedom Center was deserted and the heat of the day began to rise.

Around five minutes after ten, a woman by the name of Karen Mckernans showed up. Karen was an experienced canvasser. She was also a member of the York County Democratic Party Executive Committee. This was very unique because most executive committee members will not help a candidate during the primary. The next person to show up was Linda Dyer Hart. She brought a friend of hers as well. Linda was glowing with excitement and she was wearing the Irish O'bama shirt. Another woman came with her son. She wanted her son who was a high school student to experience first hand what politics was all about. By 10:30 a.m. we had eleven people that were ready to go. I conducted a mini canvass training in which I gave the do's and the don'ts of canvassing. I also explained that what we were doing that day was not just happening in South Carolina, but was taking place all over the country. They were serving at the front lines of a new era that was ushering its way into American Politics.

Everyone was broken up into teams of two. One of the rules of canvassing is that you should never go alone. Each person was given a list of votes that we compiled off of the VAN database. Around 11:15 a.m. all the teams were on their way out. They walked the neighborhoods talking to voters about the Senator's Iraq War Policy. These were teachers, nurses, sons, fathers, the people that the media does not cover. These voters would become the Obama Machine. They were the ones that believed there was something in Obama that could not die, the possibility of the American Dream. What also struck me the most was the fact that all of my volunteers were Caucasian women between the ages of thirty to fifty-five.

By no means am I provoking racism, but this was very uncanny in a state like South Carolina. Senator Obama was an African American male with a very strange name and South Carolina, unfortunately, is a state with a very dour past when it comes to African Americans. However, this showed me that Senator Obama was able to transcend one of the darkest layers of this country, the layer of race and racism. They walked with pride and confidence into some of the most dangerous neighborhoods in Rock Hill. I was worried for their safety. These thoughts raced through my head like a high speed train as I drove around to check on them. There was one volunteer whom I came up on that --- as I type this --- I am ashamed to say that I cannot remember her name. However, she also was reminiscent of the Kennedy Democrats from the 60's. She was progressive, brave and believed that 2007-2008 was the year of the next defining moment.

We finished canvassing around the two o'clock hour. The final count was that we knocked on over a 100 doors. I gathered all the volunteers in the executive hall at the Freedom Center. Many told their stories about the voters that they met. Some voters shared personal stories with the volunteers including a story about a friend who lost their sons and daughters in the war. Surprisingly, we received a good number of Obama volunteers.

After the discussion, I informed my volunteers of the upcoming house parties that would be taking place. I was able to sign up a few of the volunteers that were there, but this would be a challenge that I would have to face for the next three years --- trying to recruit volunteers to take up a leadership position in a campaign when they have never taken on this type of role before. The day was finally over. I felt that I had accomplished a lot especially for my area. I started to see the possibility of how Senator Obama would help change politics in South Carolina.

I called my boss, Jeremy Bird, to give him the results. I was a little nervous that he would think that knocking on 100 doors was not enough. I was still very new to which numbers were good and which numbers were bad in politics. Jeremy excitingly answered the phone and asked me how I did. "Well JB" I stated. "We knocked on 100 doors and received 35 Obama supporters" "That's awesome man!" he said. "Good work up there especially for a conservative area". I was shocked but reassured that the work I was doing in the Rock Hill Region was helping to elect Barack Obama president. At the end of the conversation, he told me to get ready for the next phase which was From Your House to the White House.

CHAPTER 4

FROM YOUR HOUSE TO THE WHITE HOUSE

House meetings was something that was very new to me. This is what I thought as I sat in my house the next day listening to Jeremy talk to the entire team on a conference call. I thought to myself, there is no way on God's green earth that South Carolinians would allow strangers in their homes. I was nervous as well as skeptical as to how this would work in South Carolina.

JB (Jeremy) explained to us that the plan was to build a team that would help first of all, elect Senator Obama president and secondly, outlast the campaign and become a leadership force on the ground. This phase would last for about two months. The strategy was to continue the one-on-ones but to add the "house meeting ask". In other words when we met with a potential volunteer we would tell them our story. Once we told them our story, we would then ask them to tell us theirs. The purpose of this was to build a personal relationship. Once that was established then the strategy of the house meeting was explained and the "ask" was made for the house meeting. Also, the members attending these meetings would consist of the volunteers social network. The volunteer who hosted the house meeting would eventually become an Obama team leader for their precinct with the house meeting guests as team members. These teams would eventually make calls, canvass and help out with GOTV (Get Out The Vote) on election day.

My first house meeting was with Linda Dyer-Hart. I figured this would be a pretty good meeting since Linda helped out tremendously with the June 9th Canvass. I also figured that we needed a good team in the Tega Cay area. I scheduled to have a one-on-one with her to discuss her house meeting. She agreed to have it and we invited thirty people to come. I was praised highly by Jeremy as one of the first field organizers to have a house meeting set up.

I checked in with Linda daily to get an update on the status of her invitees. She would inform me that her progress was going great and we could expect more attendees than we anticipated. I arrived eagerly but was also nervous at Linda's house meeting. Linda answered the door wearing her Irish-Green O'bama t-shirt. She excitedly informed me that Obama had Irish decent on his mother's side. I was shocked but not surprised to a certain extent. I walked in and was amazed to only see one person so far, Ella Scarbourgh. Ella was a very interesting person to meet. She was an African American woman in her late fifties. She was a former Charlotte City-Council Member and ran for Mayor against the incumbent, Pat McCory, but was defeated. Linda had served as her campaign manager at this time.

As time went on more people arrived, but it was not the number I expected. Seanta Clark, a physician as well as one of her friends, attended. In all, I only had five people show up. I felt like a failure once again. At the June 9th Canvass, I only turned out a small number and now I flunked my first house meeting. Nonetheless I stood up and started to give my speech on why Senator Obama should be the 44th President. I spoke about my story. I explained with passion why I left my job at Lash Group -- a job that was secure -- to work for this young Senator. I spoke about my parents and how I believed that Obama's health policies could help reduce their healthcare cost. I spoke about my hearing defect and how I admired Obama's ability to overcome great obstacles. I spoke about how Obama made feel when he announced that he was running for President. I saw his vision of a country where we could disagree without being disagreeable. I saw that perfect union that he spoke about with vigor.

I could tell after I spoke that my humble crowd of six was touched by my emotion and dedication to the Senator. I then allowed them to meet Obama themselves. I placed in the DVD player a video which explained Obama's background and his vision for America. After the video, I opened up the floor for discussion. I asked "How did the video make you feel?' What stuck out the most?" After a brief question and answer period, I then began to explain our strategy. "The purpose of these 'house meetings' is to reach the supporters' social network and build a leadership team. We believe that the best way to reach more voters is through the social network of a supporter. A supporter's social network will trust them before they trust a staff member." I also recruited two people to host a house meeting of their own and had Linda explain the simplicity of putting together a house meeting. This was the very fabric of our field program in South Carolina and would become the fabric of the Obama Campaign. These house meetings would become the GOTV teams that drove out voters in masses to make history and create the most well-equipped political campaign in all of American Politics.

I developed the confidence I needed from Linda's house meeting. Over the next couple of weeks, I conducted one-on-ones with ordinary everyday Americans. My goal in these one-on-ones was to first build leadership, secondly build a relationship and three get the potential supporter to do a house meeting.

My next one-on-one was with a young Democratic supporter named Jason Weil. This young man was full of excitement and represented the new face of urban white voters. That new face would be one that was young and moderate on a lot of issues but liberal on most. The Obama Democrat. He told me his story of how he and his wife Jeannie were married in Louisiana a little bit before Hurricane Katrina and how the destruction from the storm had a major impact on them. They had gone back through out the year to help with relief efforts. It was people like these that our campaign was looking for. Ordinary people doing extraordinary things. Jason told me he was a big supporter of

Senator Obama. Like most early supporters Jason was drawn to Obama after he gave his 2004 speech at the Democratic National Convention. He agreed to do a house meeting but he had to discuss it with his wife who was a professor at Winthrop University in Rock Hill.

When he spoke with his wife Jeannie, she agreed. Jeannie Weil was a very smart and beautiful young woman. She was very passionate about social justice issues and believed that they should be in the forefront of American society. She asked me to come and speak to her class about the Senator. I agreed to do it. I felt that this would be a good way for me to start my outreach to students. A couple of days later, I spoke with her class. I spoke mostly about the Senator's community organizing experience and his policies for college students. With no surprise, most of them were supporting him before I even arrived.

The day arrived for Jason and Jeannie's house meeting. I had been working with Jason on his invites for about a week. We were now in the month of July. It was the height of the Southern summer. Very hot and muggy, but yet beautiful. I enjoyed the vanilla skies I would witness driving on the I-77 North heading back to my home in Charlotte, North Carolina. I arrived at Jason's house around 6pm. It was a beautiful medium size Victorian home. It sat in a very prestigious moderately liberal to conservative neighborhood right down the street from Winthrop. It was known in some circles as "the neighborhood where professors live."

The house was set up perfectly for the meeting. Jeannie had the refreshments ready and the DVD was ready for the short film on Obama. By the time the meeting was ready to start, we had around 30 people in the room. This was my largest house meeting yet. There were professors from every subject in the room to hear me speak about a man that would be president. I started my presentations like many -- telling my story -- and why I gave up so much to work for a man that was unknown to the world. I put in the tape and waited for the support and excitement similar to what I received at

Linda's house meeting. To my surprise, the opposite happened.

I was peppered with questions about Iraq, health care, energy, and of course the famous issue on the economy. Being told that I have the gift of gab, I tried my best to answer these difficult questions. I quickly regurgitated all the information that I read on the website on these issues. A lot of my answers were one-liners but it satisfied their appetite for information. The floor was still open for questions when the worst thing happened. Jeannie, who was the co-host made a statement regarding the current conversation. During her statement, she said that she was still undecided.

I felt my heart drop to my feet. Here I was --- a staff member for Obama --- and one of my volunteers who was hosting a house party tells her guest she was undecided. Let's just say that I didn't receive any volunteers to host their own party. Also, because they were employees at Winthrop, many professors in the room did not want to subject themselves to signing a supporter card. Although I did not receive the support I wanted from the house party, I still was able to touch a small core of voters that would grow into a larger one.

I continued to conduct one-on-ones. I started to venture to the other counties I was responsible for. Lancaster County was very large county about 20 miles south of Rock Hill. Lancaster was a very special county in regards to its geographical location. The northern part of the county was considered a suburb of Charlotte. It was very upscale, a mixture of conservatives and liberals, and considered to be the future of Lancaster county. I held a couple of one-on-ones with local community leaders. One was Linda Blackmon-Brace. Linda was a very hard working woman. She owned her own real estate company and had a very political background. She once served on city council and tried to run for Mayor. I was surprised when I met her at the famous Jomar's restaurant in Lancaster. She already was a huge supporter of Obama. She took it upon His name was Sonny.

We had lunch and she explained to me all the things that she had done over the last month to garner support for Obama. She had held meetings in which she strategized on how to get the vote out. She also registered a good number of voters. I began to tell her about our house meeting strategy. She agreed to do one before I could finish explaining it. I was on cloud nine! I thought to myself that I had hit the jack pot when it came to volunteers. However, I would soon learn in the field of politics that many popular people in the community have a lot enemies. These made it difficult as an organizer to work with them. This would be the case with Linda.

The first person I met with in Lancaster was Mr. Lester. He was well respected in community and was part of the local NAACP. He wanted to help out with the campaign, but at the time was too busy taking care of his ailing mother. Also, he had his own health issues. He referred me to Linda Blackmon and this is how we met. A couple of weeks before July 4th, Linda hosted her house meeting. She lived in a modest house near the downtown area. I pulled up in the drive way where I noticed the Chrysler 300 with alloy wheels. On the driver and passenger door were magnets that read "Obama for President." On the front lawn she had a banner that read " Obama 08."

I entered the house and began to set up for the meeting. She had different memorabilia all over the house from past political races. She also had Senator Obama's book as well. I gave the presentation in the dining room. There were roughly fifteen to twenty people present. I conducted my presentation and at the end of it I recruited eleven people to make calls to voters each day to explain Senator Obama's plan for America.

Over the next couple of weeks, I had various house meetings. Sonny, Linda Blackmon's friend had one of his own. Because of the July 4th holiday only two people showed up. Also to our dismay the DVD player was not working. The next house meeting was conducted by a small business owner named Valerie Holley from Rock Hill. She lived in a modest community in the town of Newport. She was a single mom who owned a child daycare center.

She supported Obama because of his policy on small businesses and senior citizens. Valerie was currently taking care of her mother at the time. Her house sat in a cul-de-sac in a new development. She had the house decorated with patriotic balloons and even had a cake with a picture of the American Flag. Over twelve people attended her meeting. Most were family members from the Chester Area. The group was very apathetic and really did not trust the voting process. They referred to years past --- especially the 2000 Presidential Election. I assured them that the only way things would ever change in this country was if we became the change that we believed in. This house meeting was not one of my successful ones. No one signed up to do one of their own.

As July passed through I still had house meetings lined up with ordinary South Carolinians who had never been involved in politics before. This was the heart and soul of our campaign....ordinary people doing extraordinary things. Jeremy realized that help was needed in Rock Hill. He sent Jori Netz, a recent Furman graduate from Texas, Jeff Ingram, a recent graduate from the University of Tennessee. This was the formation of the soon to be close knit Rock Hill Obama Team.

When Jori Netz came in July of 2007, it was a breath of fresh air. It was my first time being a manager and I was ready for the task. I was also pleased because now I had company. I had someone I could organize with. Jori's first task was to learn the lay of the land in Chester and Lancaster. I took her out to Lancaster where she met Linda Blackmon-Brace and Charlene McGriff. She also went out to Chester and met with some potential supporters there. To our dismay, it was in Chester were would face one of our several encounters with racism.

One of Jori's first supporters was a young white female. I have not named her for privacy reasons. She had just moved to Chester and loved Barack Obama. Her family owned a breakfast sleep in. After their initial meeting, Jori was beside herself. She was motivated and ready to have her first house meeting as an Obama Organizer. To her dismay, her volunteer called back and told her that she couldn't have meetings there anymore. When asked about what happened, the volunteer responded by telling Jori that she had her tires slashed. She believed that the reason for the tire slashing was due to her Obama sticker. Jori was devastated simply because Chester County was very hard to organize. Along with that, it was hard to get volunteers. Jori would work hard to organize Chester and Lancaster. Her first house meeting would not pan out to be a success. Nonetheless, she fought the odds and went against the grain.

Our next task was the Presidential Debate in Charleston, South Carolina. This was an all hands on deck event. The eyes of political industry and the world were fixed on the historic city and we were in the middle of it.

CHAPTER 5

THE CALLING OF THE YOUTH VOTE

We understood that for Obama to win we needed young people to come out and vote. The first test was July 23, 2007. The RFD (Regional Field Director) for Charleston was Kevin Puelo, an intense and brilliant campaigner who started his political career in local state politics. He had the equivalent of the JFK best and brightest in the South Carolina campaign. His organizers were smart and shrewd. One was Abe Jenkins who would later become the Field Director in the general election in South Carolina. This team did a great job recruiting young people to be a part of this new political movement. They were able to recruit college students to march behind marching band with signs that read "Obama 08."

The debate was held at the Citadel. Outside, we were able to assemble a large crowd to chant Obama! This was the precursor I believe to the large involvement of young people in this campaign. Afterwards, it wasn't hard for us at all to recruit college students to form "Students for Barack Obama" groups on their campuses. The debate after party was a huge success. The Charleston Team did a great job recruiting members of my fraternity, Alpha Phi Alpha to come and do a step performance. They also recruited young children to sing as they wore Obama 08 t-shirts.

Before the debate the Senator made a stop to our Columbia Headquarters. This would the first of many times of my face to face meetings with the future 44th President. Even though we were staff members, Secret Service had to have us and the Columbia Office screened. When the Senator approached me, he asked me were I was from and what section of the state I was working in. He also placed his hand on my shoulder and told me "thank you for all that you are doing."

Most famous people are scripted and would tell you what their PR staffs rehearse them to say. However, with Senator Obama, I felt like he was genuine and that he had known me for years. After the Senator greeted me and the other staff members, he huddled us around. He told us that he was running for President not for the title or for the power of the office, but he was running because of the ordinary Americans who were left out every day and were in dire need for change. He went on to say that he did not believe in coming in second place. He believed like all of us that he would win this thing. The Senator made a few more comments and then he was on his way to the debate.

Over the next few weeks, our task was set ahead of us. Our job now was to take this movement to the young people. I assigned Jeff Ingram the task of building a Student for Barack Obama Team at Winthrop as well as Northwestern High School. I assigned Jori the same task but her job was to try to develop the same thing for Lancaster High and Chester High. I assisted Jeff with Winthrop due to the fact that we had connections there. In August, we set up table at Winthrop's annual Convocation. Convocation is a welcome back event for students and incoming Freshmen. At times there could be 1200 students there. This was a great opportunity for us to sign students up. As I think back on that day, I remember the excitement and the gravity the student had towards us. We signed up a lot of people that day. In addition to that, we were able to set up our first organizational meeting.

The next day, I worked with Jeff to begin recruiting for this first meeting. I have to admit that I enjoyed calling college students more than I did any other constituency. College students to me were a breath of fresh air. The energy they had for the Senator was contagious and I basked in catching it every chance I got. We were able to recruit sixty students to be in attendance. We held this first meeting in the Kinard Building. It was typical summer night. I remember feeling very nostalgic that night. Just being on a college campus on a night in August brought back memories of my days as a college student at the University of South Carolina. The room was filled with hungry and excited college students eager to learn about Obama and how they could get involved.

Jeff and I told our story. We spoke about what influenced us to get involved in this movement. We went around the room and asked the students what was influencing them to get involved. I was amazed to hear their reasons. For some, it was jobs. For others it was healthcare, the war in Iraq and the list just went on and on. At this meeting we recruited what would be come the leaders of Students for Barack Obama, Janelle Dunlap, Dwayne Green, and Lauren Johnson. Janelle and Lauren interned for us at the Rock Hill Obama Office. I assigned Lauren to Jeff and Janelle was assigned to help Jori with Lancaster County. Dwayne Green managed the Facebook account. All three students worked hard to build this group and were very successful.

Our task that August was to register as many high school and college students as possible. We set up tables at high school football games and on Winthrop's Campus. I enjoyed registering voters. I saw what the media and many pundits don't cover --- true politics. I have always believed that true politics is educating your neighbor about the issues, the facts about those issues, and the importance of voting.

The Campaign was full of fun and excitement. Every where we turned we found people who were excited about Senator Obama. Unfortunately, there were times that we experienced racism. As staff members, we became immune to these attacks. However, we were not immune to racism when our volunteers and interns were affected. One Saturday, we conducted a barber shop/beauty salon canvass. We went to several shops and registered a good number of voters. Lauren and Jeff went to a barber shop in Rock Hill not to far from the office. This barber shop was predominately White. When

Lauren walked in to the barber shop to register voters, the owner told her with a snarl in his voice "We don't promote that thing here! Get out!!!" Lauren was ashamed, horrified and she cried. Out of all the struggles I have experienced on the campaign, I have to say this was the worst.

Nonetheless, our student team pushed on that August and early September. We registered voters and signed up supporters. We visited Friday Night Football Games and continued to have organizational meetings on Winthrop's Campus. The biggest challenge came when I received a call from our State Director, Stacey Brayboy, that Senator Obama would be hosting a rally in Rock Hill.

I thought to myself, "Finally! We have a chance of getting close to reaching our vote goals." Also, it would be chance for us as a staff to meet the Senator. We had to act fast. As the Regional Field Director, it would be my responsibility to help find a location, pick spots as ticket locations, and make sure the field organizers were making calls to build our crowd. About a week later, we had the advance team from Chicago come to South Carolina. That is when I met Stephen Jacques. I remember him to be a very nice man. I drove him around the city and we looked at various spots to hold the Senator. He told me about his previous work on various campaigns. I was very impressed by this and it inspired me in my current work.

We were unable to find a location that could hold the rally. I came up with the idea of having the Senator come to the Freedom Center. The Freedom Center is a 65,000 square foot building located in the heart of downtown Rock Hill. Freedom Temple is the largest black church in Rock Hill. It is also the church that I attended. I figured it would be an historic event and also a great idea for the rally to be here.

We began our work. I instructed the field organizers to begin making calls. Our goal was to make 3000 calls a week. We set up about five ticket locations around the city. As the date drew closer, a woman by the name of Bumi came from the Chicago headquarters. Her job was to build a crowd for the event. Bumi was an Indian American with impressive credentials. She was shrewd, smart, direct, and strong. She had a formula that estimated the crowd size by how many tickets each location gave away. Our goal was to have 1500 people at this event.

It was a daunting task of making sure this event went well. Rock Hill in my opinion was ignored by the leader in Columbia. However, I know that the reason for this was not personal but political. This was our chance to show that the team we had in place was very productive. The day before the event was a very tiresome one. Our office was packed to the wall. We (along with our volunteers) made a dozen calls. At ten o'clock that night I received a call from my pastor, Herbert Crump. He told me that he had just received a fax from the Secret Service.

The message indicated that Senator Barack Obama would not be in attendance at tomorrow's rally in South Carolina. I assured him that there was a mistake. I also told him that I would call the head of the Advance Team. I called Steven Jacques and informed him about the fax. He was hesitant at first but then told me that it was true.

I begged and pleaded with him not to let this happen. He told me that there was nothing he could do. The Senator was called to vote on a bill that would provide funding for the Iraq war. I hung up the phone and went into panic mode.

I called Jeremy Bird and informed him about the situation. The first step was to call the church and let them know that Senator Obama was not coming. The second step was to set up a robo call to all the people who were coming. Lastly we would have the radio stations announce that the Senator was not coming. That night I was embarrassed and also I was hurt. I said to myself, "finally we were going to have a chance to accomplish our goal.

Another reason I was embarrassed was because the event was going to be held at my church. Now I had to face my church members with disgust and embarrassment. I was so embarrassed that I had my girlfriend call my parents to tell them the news. However I then realized that the value of a true leader is shown when he or she is able to bounce back from a defeat.

Jeremy called and informed me of the plan moving forward. They had begun to make over 1500 calls to the people who would be attending the event. My field organizers also made calls to their volunteers. The next day I went to Freedom Temple and waited for potential attendees to come. Our plan was to tell them that the event was canceled. The embarrassment and the fallout from the Senator not coming still weighed heavily on me. My Deputy Field Director, Nicole Price, came to help oversee the project at Freedom Temple. She informed me that the Senator would be conducting a radio interview on the Charlotte Radio Station, 97.9. I was pleased to hear that Senator Obama would call directly to the people.

Around two o'clock in the afternoon I listened to him on the radio. He eloquently explained to the listeners that he was deeply sorry that he could not come to Rock Hill. He also stated that his first job is to be a United States Senator and that he was summoned by Senate majority leader to take a crucial vote on the Iraq War. He also stated that he would be back to Rock Hill in about two weeks. Upon hearing this I felt relieved. We quickly started working on the Senator's arrival.

The plan for the next two weeks was to call everyone back who RSVP'd as well as invite new people. Stephen Jacques came back down and we secured Northwestern High School in Rock Hill. I can remember the excitement on the faces of the Principal and staff once they learned of Obama's coming. This was a great opportunity for the Rock Hill Region to increase our youth vote and youth volunteers.

Early the week of the event, I began to re-invite political leaders to have VIP seating. Among the elite were: Congressman John Spratt, Charlotte Mayor Pro Tem Patrick Cannon, Former South Carolina House Rep Sam Foster, Former South Carolina House Rep Betsy Moody-Lawrence,

Mayor of Rock Hill, and many more. Since I was the Regional Field Director for the area, I was privileged to receive Secret Service permission to meet Senator Obama. Steven asked me to pick out some people whom I wanted to take to the back to meet Obama after the event. I gave him the names and social security numbers of my parents, girlfriend and my mother's friend, Willia Truesdale.

Twenty four hours before the rally approached and everything was moving smoothly. The advance team had a head count of around 1500 people. Our office made over 3500 calls and we had a large volunteer team ready to help. Steven Jaques called and asked if I knew anyone who would be willing to pick up Senator Obama at the Rock Hill Regional Airport. I immediately gave him the name of my best friend, Paul Holmes. I called Paul and he immediately accepted. It was D-day and all our people were ready to go. The event was scheduled to start at 7:00 pm. By 4:00 pm, we had a line stretched for about a mile. We worked with the advance team to make sure that no one brought in their own signs. It was the campaign rules at rallies that attendees be given placards and not allowed to bring their own.

Senator Obama arrived around 7:05 pm. Congressman Spratt introduced him and welcomed him to his district. Obama embraced the Congressmen and took the mic. I later learned that before the event Spratt and Obama had a conversation in the back room. It was told that Obama asked Spratt for an endorsement and Spratt still refused at that time. Many said that this angered Obama, but he was able to brush it off and go out on stage. He spoke to the crowd with passion and he gave them hope. He spoke about how we can perfect our union by working together as one nation.

The event was a huge success. We filled the gym and had an overflow. We signed up over 1,000 plus potential supporters and volunteers. The next day we had the laborious task of inputting this information into the VAN. The Obama event helped our region out tremendously. As a result, my organizer over York County received enough "2"s to get him close to his vote goals. We also were able to get more volunteers like Gloria White from Clover, South Carolina and Robert Hillman from Charlotte, North Carolina.to come to the office. The end result I believe was the increase in our youth involvement which helped propel us over the finish line in January 2008.

CHAPTER 6

40 DAYS OF FAITH AND FAMILY

In South Carolina, faith is everything. Many people go to church twice a week. This is particularly true in the African American community. Throughout the Fall of 2007 we were tasked by the political shop in Chicago and Columbia to conduct a a series of faith forums throughout the state. This project was entitled "Forty Days of Faith and Family." The goals were to engage the faith community; talk about the issues people of faith find important, and share the Senator's faith with them.

In my region, I targeted key churches to conduct these meetings. We targeted two in Rock Hill and a community center in Lancaster. Marnie Robinson, our State Faith Director held a conference call with all the Regional Field Directors to lay out the logistics. The goal was to call churches in the area and ask the pastors to send a representative to the forum. We had to call all denominations, and at the same time make sure the churches we were calling were not sensitive to politics. At these forums, our National Faith Director, Joshua Dubois, and Deputy Faith Director, Paul Monterio, would preside.

I decided to have Jeff go first on the faith forum. We booked the Freedom Center once more. I felt like we had to do something there (given what had happened with the Obama Rally). On top of that, Hilary Clinton's Campaign decided to host their rally at the Freedom Center after ours fell through. We had one problem with having the Rock Hill Faith Forum at the Freedom Center. Freedom Temple was largest African American Church in York County. With this popularity came a lot of enemies. We feared that because of this jealousy many would be reluctant to come to the forum.

To avoid this, we approached our volunteer base. We e-mailed our leaders and asked them to recruit people they trusted in their congregation. We felt that if we used the same recruitment technique as the house meetings we could get better results. The first faith forum took place at Freedom Temple around noon. This was put together by Jeff. We invited as many clergymen as possible but came up with a turnout of only fifteen people. Nonetheless the discussion was very insightful. As I think back to that event, I can't remember all the names of those who attended, however, it was a diverse group. I remember there was a representative of the Muslim community in attendance. This was very good in my opinion. Although most of the public abhorred Muslims, what we wanted to show is that the Senator believed that America needed to reach out to the Muslim Community and not berate them.

Paul Monterio led a workshop entitled "My Faith, My Family, My President. In this workshop, he would ask the attendees how their faith had influenced them in their lives. He would then talk about how the Senator's faith influenced him in his life. The next part of the workshop focused on family. Paul would ask them how their faith influenced their family. I was very impressed to hear the responses of some in the audience. Many talked about how if they didn't find Jesus, they wouldn't know where they would be. Others shared stories on how their family helped to enhance their faith. The last section was called My President. Here is where we asked the audience how faith should affect the President. One woman stated that she believed that the faith of the President should help guide him or her in important decision affecting the country. However, the faith or religion of the President should not be pressed upon the American People.

After the meeting, we would then ask the audience if they would volunteer to be congregation captains. A congregation captain is responsible for recruiting members of their church to volunteer on the Obama Campaign. These volunteers would help make phone calls, canvass, and help out on Election Day. Thinking back, the York Faith Forum although small in attendance was large in impact. It was the first of its kind in the area. I believe one area where we missed a key opportunity was making more of an aggressive outreach to the Catholic and Presbyterian communities, which took place later on in the campaign after South Carolina.

Our next faith forum took place in Lancaster, which was a traditional blue collar community. It was hit hard by the closing of a major manufacturing plant called Springs. It was a very large county. It stretched from the outskirts of Charlotte, North Carolina, bordered York and Chester County; then ended at the Kershaw County line. I was worried about this one because of the history of trying to get the people of Lancaster to turn out for meetings. Along with that, there was racial tension between some of the volunteers/supporters and Jori.

A majority of our volunteers and supporters were black. Some of them felt that with Jori being a white female from Texas, that she couldn't understand what was going on in the black community. As the Regional Field Director, I was able to put out these fires. I was furious at the fact that no matter how much progress was made in race relations, we still based everything on color and not content. This would be a problem on the campaign which also would come up during the President's first year in office.

We decided to have the faith forum at a community center in downtown Lancaster. This community center was the pillar in the local black community. I remember the day of the event it rained, but to our relief, it ended as the time for the forum drew near. We expected a large turn out because of our call volume. To our dismay, only ten people showed up. I was embarrassed due to the fact that Joshua had come to do this forum. It was at this moment that I began to realize that my area was one of the most conservative parts of the state. I also realized that in order to turn people out for a

45

forum such as this one, a stronger push had to be made then what you have already put forth.

Joshua did a good job conducting the workshop. He was able to turn the negative perception of only ten people showing up to a positive perception of what those ten people could do. These faith forums took place all across the state. In my opinion, it was one of the most successful political outreach strategies to the faith community. We were able to receive endorsements from key people in the faith community, which I believed help us to beat the Clinton Campaign. The finale of the 40 Days of Faith and Family was scheduled to end with a large scale gospel concert with Pastor Donnie McClurkin as the headliner. Pastor McClurkin had family from Chester which was in my area.

To me, this was heaven sent because it would help to encourage voters in Chester to vote for Obama. This concert would also help us statewide with signing up supporters. Of course, there would be another hurdle that we would have to get over. The concert was almost derailed due to Pastor McClurkin's stance on homosexuality. Pastor McClurkin stated that he was cured by the Holy Spirit from homosexuality. This stirred up the gay community. As a result of this, the pastor stepped down from the tour. In the end, the 40 Day of Faith and Family was a success. We were able to secure thousands of supporters and new volunteers.

CHAPTER 7

THE DOUBLE O TRAIN

December 2007 was a very crucial time on the campaign. We only had one month until the South Carolina Primary. I was utterly exhausted and beyond stressed out. I had been working 80 plus hours a week and sleeping on average three to four hours a night. The stress I felt was beyond any level I had ever felt before. I can remember waking up every morning wondering if this day would be my last day on the campaign. Our numbers were good in Rock Hill but not as good as the Aiken Office which was about the same size as our office. Nonetheless we still held our own.

December was also my favorite time of the year. I love the Christmas Season. I become nostalgic this time of the year as I recollect on my childhood. However, this Christmas would be a different one. I would have to sacrifice my yearning for engulfing myself into the spirit of the season. I would have to engulf myself into Barack Obama. As the month began, Stacey told us that the "Double O Train was coming to South Carolina". I remember thinking to myself exactly what did she mean. She announced that Senator Obama, Michelle Obama and Oprah Winfery were coming to South Carolina.

The goal was to make this event the largest one on the campaign. Jeremy stated that we needed to have 25,000 people there and it would be at William-Brice Stadium. Upon hearing this I was happy, but at the same time I was not. I knew this meant that I would have to face my fear of calling both black and white voters in York, Chester and Lancaster. I knew that I would have to face a voter on the phone calling Barack Obama the "N" word. When it came to campaigns, I was terrified of making voter calls. I was well aware that calls were the heart beat of every campaign. I felt more comfortable addressing voters at a town hall meeting or going door to door. I always felt that making phone calls to voters were not personal. When you make a call to a voter, it is hard for them to see your passion. It is also hard to explain to them over the phone --- in less than three minutes --- why they should vote for your candidate. Nonetheless I knew I had to do it. My goal for my office was to go through the African American Voter Universe first and complete it. Then we would switch to calling Caucasian Women Voters. We believed that since Oprah was very popular among Caucasian Female Voters 55 and younger/older we would get a good response. As I made these calls, I thought about all the lives I would be changing if Senator Obama got elected.

This very thought alone helped me get through the calls in which I heard comments like "I am not voting for that "N" or "Is this a joke?!!! I am hard core conservative!!!" I learned to take this calls with stride. I had to realize that everyone is not going to like you and not everyone is going to like your candidate.

The big day came for the "Double O Train" to come to Columbia. It was a very mild December day in South Carolina. I spent the night before at my parent's house in Camden, which was a small town about thirty miles east of Columbia. The town is known for its horse races. Camden became my home in 1993 when I moved there from Jamaica Queens, New York. The event was held at Williams-Brice Stadium which was the cathedral of Columbia. This is where my alumni, the University of South Carolina Gamecocks, played SEC College Football. I remember arriving at the stadium around 8AM. The dew was still fresh on the ground as the sun rose over what would turn out to be a very historic day.

I walked towards the stadium to receive my assignment. My job was to work with other organizers to manage the flow of the crowd outside the stadium. We had to make sure that we signed up everyone in line. As it drew closer to the event, the atmosphere around the stadium took on the feel of a homecoming football game. The crowd was diverse. There were blacks, whites, women, men, children, high school and college students all coming together. This was historic in itself in a state that had a rocky past with race relations. It was time for the event to take place. I remember walking my parents, my mother's friend and my girlfriend in to take their seats. I assumed my position down on the football field looking up at the stage at three historical African Americans --- Michelle Obama, Senator Obama, and Oprah Winfrey.

Before the event started, Jeremy Bird and Anton Gunn took the stage. Jeremy asked everyone in the audience to take out their cell phones and call the five numbers they received to call as they walked in the gates. The purpose of this was to create the largest phone bank in the history of campaigns and we did it in one day. The crowd swelled to 29,000 the largest crowd since the campaign started at that time. It was South Carolina where the signature large crowds started for Senator Obama.

Oprah Winfrey got up from her stool and began to tell her story to the crowd. She told us why she supported Senator Obama and why this was her first time stepping out on a limb and supporting a presidential candidate. After her speech, she introduced Senator Obama to speak. The Senator gave a very inspirational speech which I believed helped put him over the top. Remember, this event took place less than a month before the South Carolina primary. As I think back to this day, I remember seeing people in the crowd with tears in their eyes as the Senator spoke. His message of hope and change was not a cliché, it was a tangible object that everyone could see but were not sure how to obtain it.

I can remember seeing people pass out. I was not sure if this was due to heat or to the Senator. The Republicans would call Obama a celebrity because people would pass out at his rallies. To us, he embodied our dreams, our hope and what we wanted the presidency to look like. The "Double O' Train" as the event was called received national media attention. The media was in awe of how the campaign was able to turn out such a large number of people to William Brice Stadium. Despite all this, the one question remained. Can all these rally attendees turn into votes?

They would soon receive their answer. The next day after the event, each office in the state was instructed to take a stack of supporter cards that were collected from the stadium. Our task was to call these potential supporters and place their information into the VAN as well ask them to volunteer on or before election day.

As the Christmas Holiday approached, all the RFD's were called down to Columbia to discuss our GOTV (Get Out The Vote) Strategy. Craig Schirmer our Early State Advisor, was in charge of this effort. At these meetings, we had to review our regions and check to see if we were close or had met our vote goals. In Rock Hill, we were close and would make them by the end of the year. Craig and Jeremy announced a GOTV Training with staff on December 30 and 31st 2007 in Columbia. The goal of this training was to get the staff and our volunteers ready for primary day. It would be at this training that I would learn the value of grassroots organizing and how important all the hard work we conducted for the past year would pay off. As I went home to Camden for the Christmas Holiday, I took time out to reflect on the campaign.

I started to ask myself what was next after this primary? Would I continue on? Would we really win? I also reflected on the history that I was helping to create. Despite this I still couldn't stop thinking to myself did I do a good job? Am I doing a good job? I asked myself these questions because although we were reaching our goals, other offices were doing better and had active volunteers. The Rock Hill Office had active volunteers but the majority of them were from Charlotte.

I began to realize two things. The Rock Hill Area was a very hard place to organize --- especially for a Democrat. It was very conservative and it was hard for local democrats to get elected. The other thing I realized is how strong the hunger for change was. The fact that volunteers from another state (North Carolina) would drive all the way to Rock Hill and Chester, South Carolina to campaign for Barack Obama was amazing in itself.

As the air turned from the mild smell of autumn to the crisp southern chill of winter, the light at the end of the tunnel started to shine. In less than a month was the Virginia Governor, Tim Kane visit. In December of 2007, Kane came and spoke to laid off textile workers. The event was a success and I believe that the Governor's moderate views resonated with the citizens of Lancaster.

My mother had the house decorated just perfect for the season. I became nostalgic all other again as I remembered my days as a child celebrating Christmas in New York. My parents were very proud of me. They knew that I was helping to make history. My grandfather, Reginald Jones, who was deceased would have been even more proud. He was from Panama and became a citizen of the United States. He fought in WWII and was a long time Roosevelt and Kennedy Democrat. The fact that I was helping to elect the country's first African American President would have made him leap for joy. I knew that I took a risk giving up a stable job to go and work on a Presidential Campaign. Little did I know at that time of the dark days that would soon come upon me for such a sacrifice. Periods of unemployment and financial woes. In the end I believe and still do that it was all worth it for the improvement of our society and our nation.

On Christmas Eve I had to get on a conference call with David Plouffe. The entire campaign from across the country was on the call. David spoke about the upcoming primaries and how proud he was of us all. He began to weep on the phone as he spoke about our dedication to this campaign. He also spoke about how proud we would feel on January 20, 2009 when would see Barack Obama raise his right hand and take the oath of office. At that time it was so hard to imagine but little did I know it would come true.

On New Year's Eve we had a training in Columbia at the YMCA. This training was held to prepare us for GOTV. Craig Schirmer, our Early State Advisor, conducted the training. He taught us how the process should go on Election Day. He told us about different roles like poll checker, poll runner, staging location director, etc. I had no idea how important creating that list of supporters --- through knocking on doors, making phone calls, and holding organizational meetings --- was to winning Election Day. It was at this time when I realized that politics is power. He even had us do a role play on how a staging location should be operated.

On January 1, 2008 we had to report back to our offices and get ready for the next 25 days. I felt like I was ready. I felt like the old way of doing politics was in our hands to show the nation that a new generation of Americans had arrived and was ready to bear the responsibility of leadership in the 21st Century. It was a very cold New Year's Day. Our office always had a distinct scent to it. It was the smell of campaign placards and dry ink from the signs volunteers had made to welcome the Senator back in September. I was very skeptical of making calls that day. I felt it was disrespectful to call voters on a holiday. What I would learn later on is that in order to win in politics you have to reach out to every voter and ask for their vote. As we made calls I was shocked at the response that we received. Voters were actually glad to hear from us. We received a lot of positive support for the Senator.

January 25, 2008 was a very busy and heart pounding day. A couple of weeks earlier, Anton Gunn had brought me into the political shop and promoted me to a Political Director for the last couple of weeks of the campaign. My job was to do faith outreach to pastors across the region. Our goal was to ask pastors if it would be okay if our supporters could call them if they needed a ride to the poll. One of my biggest achievements in this role was obtaining the endorsement of the Bishop of the AME Zion Church for the

Southeast. This was a huge achievement because the Bishop would ask all his pastors across the south to endorse the Senator.

Since we were the last early primary state, other staff from Iowa and New Hampshire descended upon South Carolina. My staff in Rock Hill expanded from three (Bobby Wesley joined us in the fall of 2007) to eight. Our roles and title changed to our GOTV roles. A field organizer from New Hampshire named Toby took over my title as RFD as I went on to be the Political Director. (Sometimes I wonder if this was a promotion based upon my merit or on something else). The office was packed with volunteers and the sound of the copier running off tons of turf for canvassing. My role for Election Day was to be a staging director for a staging location in Heath Springs which is located in Lancaster County. We all left the office in Rock Hill at 1 a.m.not knowing what the next day would bring.

CHAPTER 8

PRIMARY DAY

January 26, 2008 was a day that I believe changed the course of the 2008 Presidential Elections. Prior to the South Carolina Primary, Obama lost New Hampshire and Nevada. His only hope of doing well in the February 5th states was to win South Carolina. If Obama lost, the campaign --- in my opinion -- would be over. The media over the last four years had not given the field staff in South Carolina the credit it deserved. Despite popular opinion, Iowa did not bring the presidency to Obama. Iowa began the process but South Carolina carried it out.

Saturday January 26, 2008 was a very beautiful day. I remember leaving my house in Charlotte at 4 a.m. in the morning. I had to get to Heath Springs to the staging location. My job as staging location director was to run the location and send up the number of supporters that voted (and the ones who did not) to Toby in Rock Hill. As I continued on the 45 minute trip to Lancaster, I became nervous. We were not allowed to watch the news so I was not aware (like I am now) that the media had already showed that the possibility of Obama winning South Carolina was very high.

I opened up the staging location and my volunteers were ready to roll. We worked hard and were focused. I remembered everything that Craig taught us at the training about staying and looking cool. My cell phone coverage in the area was low so I had no idea what was happening. At 7 p.m. I received the call from Toby that we won our area and Senator Obama won the South Carolina Primary. I couldn't believe that we won. I also was shocked that we won by such a large margin. I hopped in my car (it was pitch black outside) and drove an hour down the dark South Carolina back roads to Columbia to hear Senator Obama speak. History had been made, but we would have to make more.

SECTION 3

THE NEW SOUTH

CHAPTER 9

ORDINARY PEOPLE DOING EXTRAORDINARY THINGS

The next day after the primary, we were all on a high. We were told to report back to the Columbia office. All of the staff was there plus volunteers. Jeremy spoke about what we achieved. We were able to prove that when we connect with people and inspire them to be leaders we could make change happen. I remember the flood of volunteers coming in. Many were overcome with emotions of joy with tears flowing.

Many individuals gave emotional speeches about the sacrifice they gave over the past year for Obama. Listening to these speeches I began to feel more and more that I was part of a movement beyond what anyone had seen. We changed the way politics was done, not just in the country, but in the south. We had laid a foundation for democrats to run in the south and put an end to street politics --- at least that's what I thought at the time.

Jeremy began to give our new assignments. We were to pack up and drive to the next battleground states in 48 to 72 hours. I couldn't believe this and was shocked. I was so exhausted, I could not even imagine going to another state. I weighed my options. We were given the choice of either going or jumping off the train and get on in the General Election

I decided to jump off. I was very exhausted and needed time to rest. Later I would realize that this was the worst mistake I could ever had made. I believe that not continuing through the February 5th states was the catalyst to my periods of unemployment over the next four years.

Over the next few months, I continued to follow the campaign closely as well as recuperate from the past year. I became somewhat of a local celebrity. I was invited to speak at various local political functions to help energize the base. It amazed me that the Obama name was so attached to me and followed me where ever I went. However, to my dismay, I was unemployed for the first time in a long time.

I was surviving just off of $425 a week from UI Benefits. I was unable to obtain work in the private sector because of my political background. As far as the public sector, I was still new to the game and did not develop the correct contacts that were needed to excel. I was new to this and oblivious to the fact that political campaigns are not like regular jobs. You really have to connect to the right person. I focused my energy on trying to help ordinary people do extraordinary things. Due to Obama's surprising victory in South Carolina and Iowa, many of the Obama volunteers (including my own) decided to go the extra mile and run for office themselves.

There was Pete Skidmore Sr. who was one of my most dedicated volunteers. His son, Pete Skidmore Jr., was an Iraq veteran who introduced Obama at several stops in South Carolina. Pete Sr, was a blue collar guy. He started his own private investigator business and was successful. With a background in law enforcement he decided to run for coroner of York County. He was a great match for this and I would eventually help him during the general election. I also focused on my city, Charlotte. North Carolina's primary was not until May. My goal was to try to get back on the campaign then. Because of my Obama background, I was elected chairman of precinct 243 in Southwest Charlotte. This automatically placed me on the County Executive Committee of the local Democratic Party. With this position I felt I could help the Obama Campaign win Mecklenburg County.

In February 2008, I spoke with many of the Charlotte Obama Volunteers to get them ready for the May Primary. Many of these volunteers helped out in the South Carolina

Primary by knocking on doors and making phone calls in Rock Hill, Chester, and Lancaster. Now, they were ready. We conducted meet ups, phone calls, and e-mail groups. Although I was no longer employed at the time with the campaign, I still worked hard for the Senator.

This meeting continued through the early spring. It was going well but I still could not land a job anywhere. My finances were dwindling and a lot of my bills were behind. I looked vigorously for jobs in Charlotte and all over. To my dismay, nothing came through. In April of 2008 I received a call from the South Carolina Democratic Party to help with a campaign in Florence. The Incumbent Mayor was running for re-election and was being challenged in the Democratic Primary. The mayor's challenger was a young lawyer named Steven Wukela who was a strong Obama Supporter. The Mayor, Frank Wills was a Hilary Supporter. This was a very hard decision for me.

The Mayor did not support Obama and I knew this was not going to be a win for him. Florence had a large black population and would revolt against the mayor for this. The other issue was that I lived in North Carolina and would have to commute at least 2 hours. Even though my parents lived in Camden which was 45 minutes away, I would still have to drive down from Charlotte to Camden then to Florence. In addition to this one of our former political endorsements, Leah Moody, was running for a state Senate seat which comprised of Chester and York County. She was another one that --- by Obama's winning of the primary --- decided to join the class of ordinary people doing extraordinary things.

I was asked by Leah to help advise her on her campaign. I decided to do this as well. So here I was, unemployed but making use of my time by helping former volunteers change their community by running for public office. Although Mayor Wills was not an Obama supporter, I decided to help him out as a favor to the party. Later on in April of 2008, I began to commute to Florence to help out on the Frank Wills Campaign. This campaign came as shock to me, which I will explain why later. Florence was located in the Pee Dee area of SC. It consisted of one of the strongest Obama volunteer bases aside from Charleston. When the Obama campaign office was there, there was a staff of at least 10 people, and some of best field organizers in the state were there. The mayor's opponent had a huge leg up on him.

My strategy was to split the African American vote in half and to win a majority of the white vote. I knew the African American Community would rally to Wukela because of his allegiance to Obama. In May of 2008 the Democratic Primary came to North Carolina. To my dismay, I was unable to obtain a staff position on the campaign. Nonetheless, I volunteered on Primary Day along with many of my former volunteers. It felt good -- almost normal -- to go out again with this extraordinary group of people to make sure Obama won our state. In the end the work paid off and Obama won. He was well on his way to the Democratic Nomination.

In June of 2008 I was back in Florence trying to help Mayor Wills win another term. The strategy I had in place worked but not in our favor. The African American Vote was split between the Mayor and Wukela. However, we lost votes in the white community because many of them voted in the Republican Primary. The election came literally down to one vote which went to Wukela. There was a big legal challenge over this vote that lasted into the summer. In the end Steven Wukela became the next mayor of Florence.

CHAPTER 10

GENERAL ELECTION 2008

As the Summer of 2008 continued, I couldn't help but to feel a sense of guilt. I lost the Florence race by one point. On top of this, the primaries were still going on and I was not involved. I wanted to get back involved but didn't know how. I started to feel regret. I began to ask myself, "maybe I should have traveled to Alabama back in January?" What did I do wrong?" I missed the campaign trail and felt utter regret Every time I saw the Senator's face on TV. I was still unemployed and had no where to turn.

Leah Moody also lost her primary bid. Although this was a disappointment, Leah would take what she learned from meeting voters and continue to give back. She continued to practice law and in 2012 was appointed to the USC-Columbia Board of Directors. Our work as Obama Organizers was not just to win an election but to build leaders. It became clear to me like noctilucent clouds during a warm summer night that this goal was finally coming to pass in our volunteers. It was because of this I was able take my focus off of my unemployment woes and take solace on what I had accomplished over the past year.

The Summer of 2008 was a special one. You could feel that the country was embracing for a change. Not a change in just one political party over another but a a change in how we live our lives and look at ourselves as Americans. The country still believed in the American Dream that is instilled in us as children. The country seemed to be in a hypnopompic state that would soon be awakened in November. This feeling was especially evident in North and South Carolina. In North Carolina, Lt. Governor Bev Perdue was running a great race for Governor. State Senator Kay Hagan was running one of the most disciplined and focused campaigns for U.S. Senator.

In South Carolina, our volunteer base was still organizing and many of them who won primaries were running community organized based campaigns.

As summer continued on, I traveled with my family to NY and Jamaica for family reunions. You can imagine that this was difficult for me. My finances were low and I had to rely on my family to pay for my fares. Nonetheless, members of my family looked upon me amazement and utopia. They knew that a member of the family was part of history. I was going to be part of the second New Frontier. My generation would be ones to change history along with creating our own.

In August of 2008 I received a call from one of my former primary co-workers Abe Jenkins. Abe had just been hired on as the Field Director for the Obama Campaign in South Carolina. He knew that I was eager to work in the general election. This was my chance. I was both excited and nervous. I had been off the campaign trail for a while. Did I have both the mental and physical capability to go through the laborious channels of the presidential campaign? The next day I called Kelly Adams. Kelly was hired on as the General Election Director. Kelly and I were college friends back at the University of South Carolina. She was Senator Clinton's former State Director in South Carolina. Kelly was very shrewd in politics and was tough as brass ---- a trait needed for the parsimonious and laborious world of politics. I accepted her offer. I was officially hired on as the Director of Constituency Outreach. A couple of weeks later, I took on a dual role and also served as the Deputy Field Director.

The general election team in South Carolina consisted of a combination of Senator Clinton's and Senator Obama's primary campaign staff. Trav Robertson was the State Director. A veteran of South Carolina politics and a former Bill Richardson Campaign Staffer. Trav knew everyone and had a keen sense of the lay of the land. Clay Middleton, a very impressive and dynamic man, was the OFA Political Director. Clay had such knowledge of politics. It seemed like he always had some of the most common sense answers for some of the most difficult political situations. Clay took a leave of absence form Congressman Clyburn's office to work on the campaign. Abe Jenkins was one of the best field organizers from the Charleston Office. Abe knew everyone and everyone loved Abe. Kendal Corley -- a political leader in his own right in Columbia -- made politics seem easy. He approached like an all star athlete, with pose and with precision. This was the senior staff of the Obama Campaign for Change in South Carolina.

Abe and I were responsible for roughly 20 field organizers. We believed in the field. After all, it was the South Carolina ground game from the primary that became the envy of all. As September and October went along, the atmosphere was tense. Wall Street was falling and so was all the world with it. The Great Recession was being conceived and (little did I know) in less then a month, I would become -- along with the country -- a victim of it. Despite the dark shadows of financial catastrophe that surrounded us, we worked hard to make history in South Carolina. The campaign staff relied on a skeleton budget. This was due to the fact that we were a red state. Despite our positive numbers in phone banking and door knocking, Chicago asked us to send volunteers over to my home, North Carolina. Chicago believed we had a chance there. They were right.

Our office grew as Election Day approached. Jamie Harrison, Clyburn's Floor Director, came on as a senior adviser. Jamie was one the most respected political leaders in South Carolina and Washington. He was well connected. Anton Gunn was running for the State House and received help from us as well. Our staff was ready and our volunteers were inspired. The day of immense history was soon upon us and we ready to enter a new era.

CHAPTER 11

CHANGE HAS COME TO AMERICA

November 4, 2008 finally arrived. I had been commuting from Charlotte to Columbia (and staying with my parents in between) during the course of the campaign. The night before Election Day I spent the night in Camden. I was unaware of how well Senator Obama was doing in the polls. When you work for OFA, they train you not to look at polls. So I too heeded to this training and didn't watch them. I didn't realize how well positioned we were until I looked back at the polls during the 2012 Presidential Campaign.

On November 4th I woke up around 4:50 a.m. to make the 30 minute drive to Columbia. The sun rose gently as I drove on Interstate 20. My stomach was in knots (not knowing if -- at the end of this day --- would history be made.) When I arrived at the office it had a chill to it. It was the type of early morning chill that awakens your inner spirit to face the task at hand. My job was to be in the war/boiler room. Kyle Cox was our voter builder manager. Kyle was a master statistician and knew the numbers well. He created the boiler room to have a relaxed but tense atmosphere. As the numbers came in, it looked like we had a shot to win. When the four o clock hour approached, we began to move resources around to different precincts that were underperforming. As the polls closed at 7 p.m. there were voters still waiting in line to vote.

We made sure that we had comfort captains were dispatched to those locations to provide refreshments. Some returns were coming in from all over the country showing that Obama was on a solid track to 270. What was surprising was that South Carolina was too early to call. We were all excited with the hope that we could turn this solid red state to blue for once.

Our hope was dampered in about 30 minutes when MSNBC projected John McCain the winner in South Carolina. Nonetheless, we took solace when CNN projected Barack Obama as the winner. We couldn't believe it. History had been made. Cries of joy filled the office. There was an African American woman in her 60's dancing in the spirit in the office yelling "Thank you Jesus!" As an African American male, I cannot begin to describe what I was feeling at that time. MSNBC, CNN, FOX showed Hyde Park in Chicago filling with hundreds of thousands of people to hear the President-Elect speak.

They showed Jesse Jackson and Oprah Winfrey in tears as they listened to the new President. Blacks, Whites, people from all backgrounds waived American Flags with joy and pride. Change had come to America. In the end, we lost South Carolina by nine points which was very good for a Democrat. The race in North Carolina was called for Obama a week later....the first Democrat to win that state since Jimmy Carter. As I look back I am humbled to be part of history. In the years that followed the election, I faced long periods of unemployment due to the recession. As a result I faced many financial hardships, but it was worth it all. Eventually I found employment and began to rebuild my finances.

On Inauguration Day 2009, I (along with my sister) attended the ceremony. I carried a picture of my parents who were now deceased. I wanted them to be there in spirit. Many African Americans held up pictures of their loved ones who did not live to see this day. It was a surreal moment. As I type this, I am choking up now thinking about that day.

President Obama changed America. Over the next four years many critics said he couldn't change Washington. They could not be more wrong. He highlighted issues that laid in the dark for years. He brought awareness to the inner workings of Washington and showed how it can only change if we demand it. He would be elected again in 2012. What a sight that was.

I wrote this book to tell a story. A story of how ordinary people when given a chance can do extraordinary things. That is what the President was able to do and we as a people will continue to do for years to come.

ABOUT THE AUTHOR

Douglas A Wilson is the founder of Politics is Power. Dedicated to changing the world through empowering others, Mr. Wilson has been involved in community outreach for the past 12 years. He has worked with various organizations as a youth advocate. As a public speaker, he has presented at a variety of venues. He can be relied upon to deliver informative yet substantive political commentary on topics such as Hip-Hop and Politics, civic engagement, the role of youth and minorities in politics at local, state and national levels, and the role of the African American Church in politics.

As a consultant, Douglas has worked for many local and statewide campaigns. He played a role in President Barack Obama's campaign by serving as a Regional Field Director in the South Carolina Democratic Primary and as the State Director of Constituency Outreach in South Carolina during the 2008 Presidential General Election. He is currently the Political Director for the North Carolina Democratic Party. He was appointed by Mayor Anthony Foxx of Charlotte to serve on the Charlotte Relations Committee.

He received a Bachelors of Science in Physiology from the University of South Carolina-Columbia in 2001 and his Masters in Health Administration from Pfeiffer University-Charlotte in 2005. He is currently enrolled at the

University of North Carolina-Charlotte where he is pursing a graduate certificate in Healthcare Information Technology. His posts covers politics in North Carolina, South Carolina and DC as well as policy. He resides in Charlotte, NC.